THE METAMORPHIC WOMAN

"THE JOURNEY OF TRANSFORMATION: EMBRACING THE POWER WITHIN"

ROXANNE SMITH

This book is dedicated to: My Daughter

Dear Daughter,

As you graduate from college and embark on your journey of discovering yourself, I am filled with pride and admiration for the strong and confident woman you are becoming. I have written this book, The Metamorphic Woman, with you and all the women like you in mind, who are on a journey of self-discovery and self-empowerment.

This book is a tribute to your courage, resilience, and determination to redefine yourself and create the life you want to live. I hope that as you read these pages, you will find inspiration, guidance, and a sense of empowerment as you go through transformative experiences.

To all the women who are on a similar journey, I dedicate this book to you. May it serve as a reminder that you are not alone, and that you have the strength within you to overcome any obstacle and become the best version of yourself. May God be your guidance.

With all my love and support,

Mom

TABLE OF CONTENTS

Gratitude of Appreciation

Congratulations on your decision to purchase The Metamorphic Woman book! By choosing to invest in this book, you have taken a crucial step towards self-improvement and personal growth. The Metamorphic Woman is a powerful and inspiring guide that offers valuable insights and practical tools for women who are seeking to transform their lives, find their purpose, and achieve their full potential.

This book is intended to help you with exploring the difficulties of individual change while embracing new opportunities. Whether you are seeking to build on your connections, upgrade your profession, better your health, or enhance your spirituality, The Metamorphic Woman provide transformative tools to assist you on your journey. As an author, it is fulfilling knowing that my words have resonated with readers and have the power to positively impact their lives.

It is my sincere desire that "The Metamorphic Woman" will ignite inspiration, stimulate growth, and present challenges that will aid in your personal development. Your trust and support are immensely appreciated, and I am honored to have you join me on this transformative expedition. Thank you for investing in this literary work, and I believe that it will make a valuable addition to your personal library.

Roxanne Smith

26 Motivational Quotes

1. "Embrace your uniqueness and individuality."
2. "Believe in yourself and your abilities."
3. "Set achievable goals and work towards them every day."
4. "Practice self-compassion and forgive yourself for your mistakes."
5. "Learn to communicate effectively and assertively."
6. "Develop a growth mindset and keep learning new skills."
7. "Stay true to your values and beliefs."
8. "Cultivate resilience and the ability to bounce back from setbacks."
9. "Develop a strong sense of self-awareness."
10. "Be open-minded and receptive to different perspectives."
11. "Find your passion and pursue it with enthusiasm."
12. "Learn to manage your time effectively."
13. "Develop a strong work ethic and discipline."
14. "Practice empathy and compassion towards others."
15. "Learn to deal with difficult situations and people."
16. "Develop a positive attitude and mindset."
17. "Cultivate a sense of gratitude and appreciation."

18. "Develop a strong sense of purpose and meaning in life."

19. "Set boundaries and learn to say no when necessary."

20. "Practice mindfulness and meditation."

21. "Learn to handle stress and anxiety in healthy ways."

22. "Develop a strong sense of self-confidence."

23. "Take care of your appearance and personal grooming."

24. "Stay organized and keep your life in order."

25. "Develop a sense of humor and learn to laugh at yourself."

26. "Celebrate your successes and acknowledge your progress."

At its core, The Metamorphic Woman is about empowerment and self-discovery. It invites readers to explore their own unique path to personal growth and to discover the strength and resilience within themselves. Through practical tips, and thought-provoking exercises, readers will be empowered to take control of their lives. Throughout the book, there is an accentuation on self-acknowledgment and self-love. The Metamorphic Woman encourages readers to embrace all parts of themselves, including the parts that might have been viewed as shortcomings or imperfections previously. By accepting and cherishing themselves completely, readers will want to discover their internal strengths and reveal their full potential.

The path towards self-awareness and empowerment is often challenging, but the rewards are consistently worthwhile. To aid women in their transformational journey, The Metamorphic Woman serves as a comprehensive guide that provides encouragement, direction, and motivation. This literary work is designed to equip readers with the necessary resources to construct a purposeful, meaningful, and gratifying existence. Upon finishing this book, readers will possess the tools required to cultivate a life of intention and fulfillment.

In conclusion, The Metamorphic Woman is a book for any woman who is ready to take control of her own life and create the future she wants for herself. It is a guide to personal growth, empowerment, and self-discovery, offering practical tips, and thought-provoking exercises to help readers unleash their full potential. With The Metamorphic Woman as their guide, readers will be able to transform themselves and the world around them one step at a time.

PART I

THE POWER OF MINDSET

Our mentality has the power to shape how we perceive and navigate the world around us, ultimately influencing the trajectory of our lives. It is a formidable tool that can either constrain or unleash our potential for growth and fulfillment. Lately, there has been a growing fascination with the ability to shift one's mindset and its profound effects on various aspects of our lives, including how we tackle obstacles and engage with others.

The Power of Mindset is an exploration of the correlation between mindset and personal growth and development. The book delves into the various mindsets that influence our attitudes, behaviors, and beliefs. It provides readers with the resources to adopt a growth mindset and unleash their full potential. The strategies and insights presented can assist in improving relationships, advancing careers, and leading a more satisfying life. Whether seeking personal or professional growth, The Power of Mindset offers readers valuable tools for achieving their aspirations.

CHAPTER ONE

HOW MINDSET CAN INFLUENCE PERSONAL GROWTH AND DEVELOPMENT

Have you ever pondered over why some individuals seem to accomplish their objectives with ease, while others encounter difficulties despite their diligent endeavors? The solution can be found in their mindset, which encompasses a set of beliefs, attitudes, and assumptions that shape their perspective, understanding, and environment. There are two main types of mindsets: a fixed mindset and a growth mindset.

The idea that our abilities and attributes are inherent characteristics that cannot be altered is what defines a fixed mindset. Fixed-minded people tend to shy away from challenges, give up easily when faced with difficulties, and feel threatened by other people's success. They may also interpret feedback or criticism as a reflection of their inherent flaws rather than an opportunity for growth.

A growth mindset is distinguished from a fixed mindset in that it involves the belief that our skills and qualities can be developed and improved with perseverance, hard work, and dedication. Adopting a growth mentality involves approaching challenges with an open mind, persisting through obstacles with determination, and embracing feedback or criticism as opportunities for positive development.

The significance of mindset in one's personal growth and development is immeasurable. Studies have revealed that individuals who possess a growth mindset tend to embrace novel challenges, learn from their errors, and cultivate tenacity in confronting adversity. Conversely, those with a fixed mindset tend to shy away from challenges, surrender quickly, and encounter reduced levels of contentment and life fulfillment.

Additionally, mindset can shape our convictions regarding our potential for triumph. Individuals who possess a fixed mindset are inclined to perceive success because of innate aptitude or intellect, whereas those with a growth mindset maintain that success arises from diligence and persistence.

Fortunately, mindset is not set in stone. We can cultivate a growth mindset by intentionally shifting our beliefs and attitudes towards challenges, failure, and success. For example, we can embrace challenges as opportunities for growth, view failure as a necessary step on the path to success and celebrate the success of others as inspiration for our own growth and development.

To sum up, mindset is a crucial factor in personal growth and development. By adopting a growth mindset, we can surmount challenges, cultivate resilience, and attain our objectives. As we progress through subsequent chapters and delve deeper into the power of mindset, we will uncover pragmatic techniques for fostering a growth-oriented mindset and unlocking our maximum potential. With an understanding of the significance of mindset in personal development, let us now examine some practical suggestions for cultivating a positive and growth-oriented mindset.

CHAPTER TWO

TIPS FOR DEVELOPING A POSITIVE AND GROWTH-ORIENTED MINDSET

Now that we understand the importance of mindset in personal growth and development, let's explore some practical tips for cultivating a positive and growth-oriented mindset.

1. Embrace Challenges as Opportunities for Growth.

Challenges are a natural part of life, but they can be intimidating and overwhelming. Instead of avoiding challenges, embrace them as opportunities for growth and development. Approach challenges with a positive attitude and focus on what you can learn from them.

2. Regard Failure as a Crucial Phase Towards Achieving Success.

Failing is a natural facet of the learning process. Rather than interpreting it as a reflection of your competency or worth, consider it as a crucial step towards success. Use failure as an opportunity to enhance your knowledge and development, and do not hesitate to give it another shot.

3. Foster a Passion for Learning.

Learning is a continuous process, and it plays a pivotal role in personal development and growth. Foster a passion for learning by seeking out novel experiences, exploring uncharted topics, and acquiring fresh skills. Embrace your inquisitiveness and approach novel challenges with an open mindset.

4. Engage in Self-Compassion.

Self-compassion involves treating yourself with kindness, empathy, and acceptance. It implies acknowledging that you are human and bound to make mistakes. Instead of criticizing yourself for your shortcomings, offer yourself the same kindness and support that you would offer a close friend.

5. Surround Yourself with Positivity

To strengthen a mindset that is focused on growth, it can be beneficial to create a positive environment around you. This involves seeking the company of friends and family members who offer support and encouragement, while distancing yourself from those who inject negativity or criticism. Moreover, deliberately concentrate on the positive aspects of your life and express appreciation for the blessings you have received.

6. Practice Mindfulness

Being present in the current moment and concentrating on the present is the essence of mindfulness. This can assist you in staying anchored and focused, particularly during stressful or uncertain periods. You can practice mindfulness by engaging in activities such as meditation, deep breathing, or taking a few minutes to concentrate on your breathing and the feelings in your body.

7. Set Realistic Goals and Track Your Progress

To maintain motivation and concentration on your personal development, it is helpful to establish practical objectives. This entails dividing larger goals into smaller, attainable milestones, and monitoring your advancement as you go. Acknowledge and commemorate your accomplishments while also viewing setbacks as chances for education and advancement.

Ultimately, cultivating a positive and growth-oriented mindset is essential for personal growth and development. By embracing challenges, viewing failure as a necessary step on the path to success, cultivating a love of learning, practicing self-compassion, surrounding yourself with positivity, setting realistic goals, and practicing mindfulness, you can develop a mindset that will help you to overcome obstacles, develop resilience, and achieve your goals.

PART II

SELF-AWARENESS AND SELF-DISCOVERY

Welcome to the expedition of self-discovery and self-awareness! In this chapter, we will delve into the depths of our inner selves and embark on a voyage of self-discovery. Self-discovery is the process of gaining insight and knowledge about oneself, including one's personality traits, values, beliefs, strengths, weaknesses, desires, and overall identity. It involves introspection, reflection, and self-awareness, often through activities such as journaling, meditation, therapy, or trying new experiences. Self-discovery can help individuals better understand themselves, their motivations, and their purpose, leading to personal growth, fulfillment, and a more meaningful life.

Self-awareness is the gateway to unlocking our genuine potential, and comprehending ourselves on a profound level can assist us in traversing through life with a clearer objective and enhanced contentment.

This book endeavors to steer you towards a deeper comprehension of yourself, your principles, and your convictions. By obtaining a better insight into who you are, you can make more intentional decisions and lead a life that resonates with your authentic self.

Whether you aspire to conquer personal obstacles, enhance your relationships, or discover a greater sense of purpose, the perspectives and tools introduced in this chapter can aid you on your journey. Hence, join me on this expedition of self-discovery, and let us discover the concealed veracities within ourselves together.

CHAPTER THREE

THE IMPORTANCE OF SELF-AWARENESS AND SELF-DISCOVERY

Self-awareness and self-discovery are critical components of personal growth and development. They entail comprehending our identity, desires, and principles. By being self-aware, we can identify our strengths and weaknesses, our preferences, and our emotional triggers. In contrast, self-discovery involves investigating our inner selves, including our thoughts, emotions, and experiences, to achieve a more profound understanding of ourselves and our position in the world.

The importance of self-awareness and self-discovery cannot be overstated. Here are some reasons why:

1. Personal Growth: When we are self-aware, we can identify areas for personal growth and take steps to improve ourselves. This could involve learning new skills, changing our behavior, or exploring new interests. Self-discovery helps us understand what we want from life and what our purpose is. It allows us to set goals and make plans that align with our values and beliefs.

2. Better Relationships: Self-awareness and self-discovery are also essential for building better relationships with others. When we understand our own needs and emotions, we can communicate them more effectively to others. This helps us build stronger connections with people and avoid misunderstandings and conflicts.

3. Improved Decision Making: Knowing ourselves well helps us make better decisions. When we are aware of our values, beliefs, and goals, we can make choices that align with them. This helps us avoid decisions that are based on other people's expectations or societal norms.

4. Better Mental Health: Self-awareness and self-discovery are important for maintaining good mental health. When we are in touch with our emotions and thoughts, we can identify and address issues before they become bigger problems. This includes managing stress, anxiety, and depression.

5. Authenticity: Finally, self-awareness and self-discovery are essential for living an authentic life. When we know who we are and what we want, we can live our lives on our terms. This implies staying loyal to our genuine selves and refraining from compromising our values or convictions for the benefit of others.

Lastly, self-awareness and self-discovery are critical for personal growth, better relationships, improved decision making, good mental health, and living an authentic life. Taking the time to understand ourselves better and explore our inner selves can be a challenging but rewarding journey. However, it is a journey that is well worth taking. By doing so, we can become more self-aware, more self-assured, and more fulfilled in life.

CHAPTER FOUR

SELF-AWARENESS TECHNIQUES AND EXERCISES

Self-awareness plays a pivotal role in personal growth, development, and success. It entails the capacity to acknowledge and comprehend one's own thoughts, emotions, and behaviors, enabling one to pinpoint strengths and weaknesses and discern how their actions affect those around them.

Fortunately, there are various techniques and exercises that can aid in the cultivation and enhancement of self-awareness. In this chapter, we will delve into some of the most effective approaches for improving self-awareness and fostering a more profound comprehension of oneself.

Section 1: Mindfulness Practice

Mindfulness practice is a widely recognized and valuable approach, involving the direction of attention to the present moment and the non-judgmental observation of one's thoughts, emotions, and physical sensations.

There are various mindfulness techniques available, including:

a. Mindful Meditation

b. Body Scan Meditation

c. Walking Meditation.

1. Mindful meditation involves sitting comfortably and focusing on the breath or a specific mantra to calm the mind and increase awareness of thoughts and emotions.

2. Body scan meditation entails lying down and gradually scanning the body from head to toe, being mindful of any sensations or tension.

3. Walking meditation involves walking slowly and mindfully, focusing on each step and being aware of the sensations in the body, promoting relaxation and increasing self-awareness.

Section 2: Journaling

Journaling is another powerful tool for increasing self-awareness. By writing down thoughts and feelings, one can gain a better understanding of their inner world and identify patterns or triggers that may be influencing their behavior.

Some journaling prompts to consider include:

1. What is the current emotion I am experiencing and what is the reason behind it?

2. What are my goals, and what steps can I take to achieve them?

3. What are my values, and how can I live in alignment with them?

Section 3: Self-Reflection Exercises

Self-reflection exercises can help increase self-awareness by encouraging individuals to examine their behavior and thought patterns.

Some self-reflection exercises to try including:

1. One technique for identifying the root cause of a particular behavior or feeling is called the 5 Whys. Simply ask yourself "why" five times to get to the underlying issue. For example, if you're feeling stressed, start with "Why am I feeling stressed?" and then ask "why" four more times until you reach the root cause. For instance, "Because I have a lot of errands to run," "Why do I have a lot of errands to run?" "Because there is no other way I can get what I need," "Why didn't you ask someone to help split the errands with you?" and so on.

2. Feedback Analysis: Take time to reflect on a recent experience and make note of your accomplishments, areas where you could have improved, and the lessons you learned from the experience.

3. Mind Mapping: Use a visual representation to organize your thoughts and ideas by starting with a central concept and then branching out with related ideas and thoughts.

Section 4: Social Interaction

Finally, social interaction can also increase self-awareness by providing feedback and different perspectives.

Some social interaction exercises to consider include:

1. Seeking Feedback: Ask trusted friends or colleagues for feedback on your behavior, communication style, or performance.

2. Role-Playing: Practice a challenging conversation or situation with a trusted friend or colleague to gain insight into your behavior and communication style.

3. Group Discussions: Participate in group discussions or debates to hear different perspectives and challenge your own beliefs and assumptions.

Finally, personal growth and development are significantly enhanced by possessing self-awareness as a fundamental skill. One can enhance self-awareness and obtain a better comprehension of their thoughts, feelings, and behaviors by utilizing techniques like mindfulness practices, self-reflection exercises, journaling, and social interaction. Furthermore, these methods can lead to the development of greater empathy, communication abilities, and an overall sense of well-being.

PART III

EMBRACING CHANGE AND TAKING RISKS

Change is an unavoidable part of life, and it can be a difficult road to navigate. Even if we recognize that change is necessary for growth and progress, we may still feel afraid, uncertain, or resistant to it. However, accepting change and taking chances can serve as a potent force for both personal and professional advancement.

The subsequent chapters will cover the topic of embracing change and taking risks in order to achieve our goals and aspirations. It will delve into the reasons why change is essential, the advantages of taking risks, and strategies for overcoming fear and resistance to change. You will learn about building resilience, developing adaptability, and cultivating a growth mindset to help you navigate change and make informed decisions about risks. Furthermore, we will explore the importance of failure and how it can provide valuable lessons for growth and development.

Whether you're pursuing a career shift, embarking on a new project, or seeking out new experiences, you will learn how to acquire the tools and mindset required to confidently and resiliently embrace change and take risks.

CHAPTER FIVE

RISK TAKING IN PERSONAL GROWTH

Risk-taking is a vital component of personal growth and development. It involves stepping outside of one's comfort zone, taking chances, and facing the possibility of failure or uncertainty. When we take risks, we expose ourselves to new experiences, perspectives, and opportunities, which can lead to personal and professional growth.

In this chapter, we will explore why risk-taking is essential for personal growth and the benefits it can provide.

Section 1: Growth Mindset

Having a growth mindset means believing that through hard work, effort, and dedication, one's abilities and talents can be developed. This mindset is crucial when it comes to taking risks because it helps us see challenges as chances for growth and learning. By adopting a growth mindset, we become more inclined to take risks because we recognize that failure is not a reflection of our capabilities, but rather an opportunity to learn and enhance ourselves.

Section 2: Building Confidence

Assuming risks can contribute to the development of confidence and self-esteem. When we take a chance and succeed, we experience a sense of accomplishment and pride in our abilities, which can increase our confidence and motivate us to pursue more risks in the future. On the other hand, even if we fail, taking risks can still be advantageous for boosting confidence. Through taking risks and experiencing failure, we learn that setbacks are not permanent, and we can recover and try again.

Section 3: New Opportunities

Assuming risks can open doors to new prospects for personal growth and development. When we push beyond our comfort zone, we expose ourselves to novel experiences, perspectives, and possibilities. These experiences can lead us to cultivate new interests, passions, and abilities that we may not have encountered otherwise.

Section 4: Overcoming Fear

Taking risks is frequently impeded by fear, which can be the most substantial obstacle. The apprehension of failure, the unknown, and rejection can prevent us from pursuing our aspirations and seizing opportunities. Nonetheless, we can conquer fear and take risks with confidence by embracing it and using it as a motivating factor. By identifying when fear is limiting us and implementing techniques such as positive self-talk, visualization, and mindfulness, we can overcome it.

In summary, the act of taking risks is a fundamental aspect of personal growth and advancement. It necessitates venturing beyond our comfort zone, embracing uncertainty and confronting the prospect of failure. Nevertheless, the advantages of taking risks, such as enhancing self-assurance, uncovering novel prospects, and conquering fear, can be priceless in both our personal and professional lives. By adopting a growth-oriented mindset and embracing fear, we can develop the ability to take risks confidently and accomplish our aspirations and ambitions.

CHAPTER SIX

STRATEGIES FOR OVERCOMING FEAR AND RESISTANCE TO CHANGE

Overcoming fear and resistance to change can be a challenge as they often hinder our ability to embrace new experiences or opportunities. However, there are effective strategies that can help us move forward towards personal growth and development. Some of these strategies are examined in this chapter.

Section 1: Overcoming Fear

This section focuses on the importance of identifying the source of our fear as the first step in overcoming it. By understanding what is causing our fear or resistance to change, we can develop a plan to address it effectively. To begin this process, we can ask ourselves questions such as:

- What is the underlying reason for my fear?
- What factors are preventing me from making this change?
- What are the potential benefits and drawbacks of this change?

By identifying the source of our fear and resistance, we can take the necessary steps to overcome it and move forward towards our goals.

Section 2: Underlining Factors of Fear

- What is the underlying reason for my fear?
  a. Fear can be a powerful and overwhelming emotion that can impact our thoughts, behaviors, and overall well-being. However, it is important to identify the underlying reasons behind our fears in order to properly address and overcome them. Understanding the root cause of our fear can help us develop effective coping mechanisms and strategies to manage and eventually diminish its hold on us. Whether it stems from a past traumatic experience, an irrational belief or assumption, or a fear of the unknown, acknowledging and exploring the source of our fear can be a crucial step towards our personal growth and emotional healing. By facing our fears head-on and understanding their underlying reasons, we can reclaim our power and live more fulfilling and authentic lives.

- What factors are preventing me from making this change?
  b. Making a change when it comes to fear can be a challenging and daunting task. Many factors can prevent us from taking the necessary steps to overcome our fears, such as our mindset, envi-

ronment, and support system. Negative thought patterns, limiting beliefs, and self-doubt can all contribute to our reluctance to confront and overcome our fears. Our immediate surroundings and the people we surround ourselves with can also play a significant role in our ability to make change, as they can either encourage or discourage our efforts. Lack of support or understanding from others can make us feel isolated and powerless, further hindering our progress. It is important to recognize and address these factors in order to create a positive and supportive environment that fosters growth and change. With the right mindset, support, and tools, we can break free from the grip of fear and live the life we truly desire.

- What are the potential benefits and drawbacks of this change?

  c. Introducing changes in our lives can have advantages and disadvantages. On the one hand, it can offer fresh opportunities, novel experiences, and individual development. It may aid us in surmounting obstacles, acquiring new abilities, and fostering a feeling of achievement and self-assurance. Moreover, modifying our circumstances can result in enhanced connections, a superior equilibrium between work and personal life, and a heightened sense of contentment and satisfaction.

Change can be demanding and discomforting and may carry inherent downsides. While undergoing a transformation, we may be confronted with unease, uncertainty, and self-doubt, as well as resistance from individuals who are content with the status quo. Additionally, change may entail significant physical and mental exertion, a substantial time commitment, and the allocation of resources, all of which can prove challenging to manage. Consequently, it is imperative to carefully assess the potential benefits and drawbacks of pursuing change, and to develop a thoughtful plan and a reliable support system to help us overcome any obstacles that may arise.

Section 3: Challenge Negative Thinking

Negative thinking can contribute to fear and resistance to change. When we tell ourselves that we cannot do something or that we will fail, we are more likely to feel afraid and avoid taking risks.

To overcome negative thinking, we can practice reframing our thoughts. Instead of focusing on the potential risks or negative outcomes, we can focus on the potential rewards and positive outcomes. We can also remind ourselves of past successes and use positive affirmations to build our confidence.

Section 4: Change Your Perspective

Our ability to embrace change is influenced by our perception of it. It's crucial to acknowledge that change is a natural and inescapable aspect of life, and it can lead to personal growth and positive results. In this section, we'll examine various methods for altering our outlook on change. One effective strategy is to focus on the potential benefits of the change rather than the risks. This can involve creating a list of all the positive outcomes that could result from the change, and reminding ourselves of them when we feel fearful or resistant.

Another strategy is to reframe the change as an opportunity for growth and development. Instead of viewing the change as a threat, we can see it as a chance to learn new skills, gain new experiences, and expand our horizons.

Section 5: Take Action

Taking action is a crucial step in overcoming fear and resistance to change. By actively working towards our goals, we can build confidence and overcome our fears. In this section, we will explore some strategies for taking action.

A useful tactic is to begin with modest beginnings. By taking incremental strides towards our objectives, we can progressively enhance our self-assurance and conquer our apprehensions. This may require establishing minor objectives or dividing bigger goals into more feasible duties.

Another strategy is to seek support from others. Having a supportive network of friends, family, or colleagues can provide us with encouragement and motivation to overcome our fears and take action towards our goals.

Through the application of these tactics, we can conquer our anxieties and reluctance towards change, and make progress towards our individual advancement and improvement.

Section 6: Start Small

Taking small steps towards change can help us overcome fear and resistance. Starting small allows us to build our confidence and develop the skills and mindset needed to make more significant changes.

For example, if we are afraid of public speaking, we can begin by speaking in front of a small group of friends or family members. As we become more comfortable, we can gradually increase the size of our audience and take on more significant speaking opportunities.

Section 7: Seek Support

Overcoming fear and resistance to change can be aided by seeking support from others. Seeking out a trusted friend, family member, or mentor can offer us valuable feedback, guidance, and encouragement. Additionally, seeking professional assistance from a coach or therapist can equip us with the necessary skills and mindset to address our fear and resistance to change.

Section 8: Strategies for Overcoming Fear

Numerous effective tactics exist to aid us in conquering our apprehensions and reluctance towards change. One such approach is to confront our fears directly.

a. Confront Our Fears

By directly facing the object of our anxiety, we can gradually boost our assurance and lessen our stress.

b. Relaxation Techniques

Additionally, engaging in relaxation techniques, such as deep breathing, meditation, or yoga, can help us regulate our physical and emotional reactions to fear and decrease our stress levels. These methods can facilitate our ability to cope with and manage change effectively.

c. Seek Support

Seeking support from others can be a powerful tool in overcoming fear. Talking to friends, family, or a therapist about our fears can provide us with encouragement and validation, as well as help us gain a different perspective on the situation. It is also important to be kind and compassionate towards ourselves and to recognize that change can be difficult, but it is an opportunity for growth and learning.

d. Formulate a Plan

Finally, developing a plan of action can help us move forward towards our goals despite our fears. Breaking down our goals into small, manageable steps and celebrating each accomplishment along the way can help us build momentum and confidence. With these strategies, we can learn to overcome our fears and embrace change in our lives.

In summary, personal growth and development necessitate the difficult task of overcoming fear and resistance to change. It requires identifying the source of our fear, challenging negative thoughts, starting with small steps, and seeking support. This process can help us embrace change and approach risks with confidence and resilience. By developing these strategies, we open ourselves up to new opportunities and experiences that can aid in reaching our full potential.

PART IV

BUILDING SELF-CONFIDENCE AND SELF-ESTEEM

Self-confidence and self-esteem are critical components of personal growth and development. When we have elevated levels of self-confidence and self-esteem, we are more likely to take risks, pursue our goals, and navigate challenges with resilience.

In this chapter, we will explore some effective strategies for building self-confidence and self-esteem.

Section 1: Identify Your Strengths

Identifying our strengths is an essential first step in building self-confidence and self-esteem. We can begin by making a list of our talents, skills, and positive qualities. Reflecting on our past successes and achievements can also help us identify our strengths.

By focusing on our strengths, we can develop a sense of pride and confidence in ourselves, which can help us navigate challenges and pursue our goals with determination.

Section 2: Set Realistic Goals

Establishing achievable objectives can aid in the development of self-confidence and self-esteem. When we establish realistic goals and strive towards them, we cultivate a sense of achievement and self-respect.

However, it is crucial to set goals that are both challenging and achievable. If we set objectives that are too arduous or unattainable, we may become disheartened and lose trust in ourselves.

Section 3: Practice Self-Compassion

Practicing self-compassion is another important strategy for building self-confidence and self-esteem. Self-compassion involves treating ourselves with kindness, understanding, and forgiveness.

When we practice self-compassion, we are less likely to be self-critical or judgmental. Instead, we can acknowledge our mistakes and failures without letting them define us. This can help us develop a more positive self-image and increase our self-esteem.

Section 4: Embrace Failure

Experiencing failure is inherent in the process of learning, and it plays a vital role in shaping our self-assurance and self-respect. Each time we fail, we gain a chance to learn from our errors and cultivate our ability to endure difficulties.

Rather than perceiving failure as a setback, we can adopt a mindset that welcomes it as a prospect for advancement and education. By examining our failures, we can formulate techniques to enhance our performance and surmount challenges that may arise in the future.

Section 5: Practice Self-Care

Prioritizing self-care is crucial in the development of self-esteem and self-assurance. Attending to our emotional and physical needs can promote a sense of positivity, resilience, and confidence.

Engaging in self-care can involve a variety of activities, including exercise, meditation, spending quality time with loved ones, or pursuing enjoyable hobbies and interests. By making our well-being a priority, we can foster a more favorable self-perception and elevate our self-esteem.

In conclusion, developing self-confidence and self-esteem is a continuous journey that demands commitment and effort. By recognizing our strengths, establishing achievable objectives, demonstrating self-kindness, embracing failure, and prioritizing self-care, we can cultivate a constructive self-perception and enhance our confidence and resilience. These approaches can enable us to tackle obstacles, strive towards our aspirations, and attain individual progress and advancement.

CHAPTER SEVEN

THE CONNECTION BETWEEN SELF-ESTEEM AND SELF-CONFIDENCE

The relationship between self-esteem and self-confidence has been widely studied in both psychology and self-improvement literature. Although the terms self-esteem and self-confidence are often used inter-changeably, they are separate constructs with unique meanings.

Self-esteem refers to how much an individual values and respects themselves. It is the overall assessment of a person's self-worth, and it encompasses their beliefs about their abilities, qualities, and traits. Self-esteem is shaped by a person's experiences, achievements, and relationships, and it can fluctuate over time.

In contrast, self-confidence is the conviction in one's aptitude to perform a particular duty or accomplish a specific objective. It is the guarantee that one can progress and succeed in a particular area. Self-confidence is contingent on the circumstance and can fluctuate depending on the assignment or hurdle involved.

The relationship between self-esteem and self-confidence is that they are interdependent, and one can influence the other. When a person has high self-esteem, they are likely to have high self-confidence in their abilities to achieve their goals. On the other hand, when a person has low self-esteem, they are likely to have low self-confidence and doubt their abilities.

Individuals possessing high self-esteem typically exhibit greater levels of confidence, assertiveness, and resilience. They are prone to taking risks, remaining persistent in the face of obstacles, and bouncing back from setbacks. They hold a firm self-image and possess an unwavering belief in their capacity to surmount challenges and attain their objectives. Conversely, individuals with low self-esteem often question themselves, experience insecurity, and struggle with self-doubt. They may shy away from challenges and prospects for fear of failure, and they may confront feelings of anxiety and depression.

Elevating self-esteem can result in a favorable influence on enhancing self-confidence. Individuals often demonstrate increased assurance in their abilities and feel better equipped to achieve their objectives as they foster a positive self-image. Similarly, boosting self-confidence can also enhance self-esteem. As individuals achieve their goals, they experience a sense of accomplishment and gratification, which can enhance their overall sense of worth and self-esteem.

In conclusion, self-esteem and self-confidence are related concepts that are essential to personal growth and development. They are interdependent, and one can influence the other. By improving both self-esteem and self-confidence, individuals can develop a stronger sense of self and increase their chances of achieving their goals and living fulfilling lives.

CHAPTER EIGHT

SELF-ESTEEM AND SELF-CONFIDENCE TIPS AND EXERCISES

Improving your self-esteem and self-confidence is a process that requires intentional effort and practice. Here are some tips and exercises that can help you boost your self-esteem and self-confidence:

1. Cultivate self-compassion: By extending to yourself the same kindness and empathy you would provide to a friend. When you make mistakes or experience setbacks, be gentle with yourself, and remember that everyone makes mistakes.

2. Celebrate your strengths: Make a list of your strengths, skills, and achievements. Focus on your positive qualities and what you have accomplished in your life. Celebrating your strengths can help you feel more confident and prouder of yourself.

3. Challenge negative self-talk: Negative self-talk can undermine your self-esteem and confidence. When you notice negative thoughts, challenge them with positive affirmations or counterarguments. Replace "I can't" with "I can try" or "I'm not good enough" with "I am worthy and capable."

4. Set achievable goals: Formulating attainable goals can bolster your confidence and self-esteem. Begin with smaller targets and gradually progress towards larger ones. Commend your accomplishments and advancements as you move forward.

5. Prioritize self-care: Nurturing your physical, emotional, and mental well-being is imperative in cultivating self-esteem and confidence. Ensure you get sufficient sleep, engage in regular exercise, maintain a healthy diet, and pursue activities that bring you contentment and peace.

6. Try new things: Stepping out of your comfort zone and trying new things can help you build confidence and self-esteem. Whether it's taking a new class, trying a new hobby, or exploring a new place, embracing new experiences can help you grow and learn more about yourself.

7. Practice visualization: Visualize yourself succeeding in a particular task or situation. Imagine yourself feeling confident, capable, and proud of yourself. This exercise can help you overcome self-doubt and build confidence.

8. Seek support: Surround yourself with people who support and encourage you. Talk to a trusted friend, family member, or therapist about your struggles and feelings. Having a support system can help you build resilience and confidence.

To summarize, enhancing your self-esteem and self-assurance is a process that necessitates patience, perseverance, and self-kindness. By integrating these recommendations and activities into your everyday regimen, you can cultivate a more robust sense of self and attain your objectives with increased poise and confidence.

PART V

OVERCOMING OBSTACLES AND CHALLENGES

Life is full of challenges and obstacles that can test our perseverance, resilience, and strength. These difficulties can come in the form of personal setbacks, professional hurdles, or global crises, and they can be overwhelming and stressful to navigate. However, overcoming these obstacles is a crucial aspect of personal growth and development. It can help us cultivate resilience, develop new skills, and strengthen our sense of self. This chapter is designed to guide you through the process of overcoming challenges and obstacles, and to help you navigate life's ups and downs with greater ease and confidence necessary to triumph over obstacles and challenges and lead a more fulfilling life.

CHAPTER NINE

OBSTACLES AND CHALLENGES IN PERSONAL GROWTH AND DEVELOPMENT

Personal growth and development are essential for leading a fulfilling and meaningful life. However, the journey towards personal growth and development is often fraught with obstacles and challenges that can hinder our progress and make us feel stuck or discouraged. Here are some common obstacles and challenges in personal growth and development, and how to overcome them:

1. Fear:

Fear of the unknown, fear of failure, and fear of rejection can hold us back from taking risks and pursuing our goals. To overcome fear, it's important to acknowledge and accept your fears, but not let them control your actions. Take small steps towards your goals, and gradually build up your confidence and courage.

2. Self-doubt:

Self-doubt can undermine our self-esteem and confidence and make us doubt our abilities and worth. To overcome self-doubt, challenge negative self-talk with positive affirmations, focus on your strengths and achievements, and seek support and encouragement from others.

3. Lack of direction:

Without a clear sense of direction, it can be challenging to know what steps to take towards personal growth and development. To overcome this obstacle, take time to reflect on your values, interests, and goals. Create precise and attainable objectives and divide them into feasible tasks.

4. Procrastination:

Putting things off can impede our progress towards our objectives and result in sentiments of regret and dissatisfaction. To conquer procrastination, divide tasks into more achievable segments, establish a regular schedule, and establish responsibility by setting deadlines or seeking assistance from others.

5. Resistance to change:

Change can be uncomfortable and challenging, and we may resist it even when it is necessary for personal growth and development. To overcome resistance to change, identify the benefits and drawbacks of staying in your current situation versus making a change. Focus on the benefits of change and take small steps towards it, even if it feels uncomfortable at first.

6. Lack of support:

Personal growth and development can be challenging, and it is important to have a support system of friends, family, or professionals who can offer guidance and encouragement. To overcome a lack of support, seek out resources and communities that align with your goals and interests.

To summarize, hindrances and difficulties are an inescapable component of individual advancement and improvement. By acknowledging and tackling these obstacles, we can acquire the fortitude, abilities, and outlook required to conquer them and accomplish our objectives. By demonstrating perseverance, self-awareness, and receiving support, we can manage the challenges of personal growth and development and lead a more gratifying life.

CHAPTER TEN

STRATEGIES FOR OVERCOMING OBSTACLES AND MOVING PAST CHALLENGES

Obstacles and challenges are a natural part of life and can often feel overwhelming and discouraging. However, there are strategies and techniques that can help us overcome obstacles and move past challenges. Here are some strategies to help you overcome obstacles and move forward:

1. Cultivate a Growth Mindset: Embrace the notion that with perseverance and effort, we can enhance our skills and capabilities. A growth mindset allows us to perceive challenges as chances to develop and gain knowledge. We prioritize the journey over the destination, and regard setbacks as occasions to acquire experience and progress.

2. Establishing Realistic Goals: This is a critical component in surmounting difficulties and hurdles. By dividing larger goals into smaller, achievable steps and recognizing progress along the way, you can maintain your drive and concentration, even in the face of obstacles or setbacks.

3. Seek Support: Don't be afraid to ask for help and support when facing obstacles or challenges. Reach out to friends, family, or professionals who can offer guidance and encouragement. Join a support group or community related to your goals or interests.

4. Prioritizing Self-Care: Self-Care is crucial for surmounting obstacles and transcending challenges. Dedicate time to self-care pursuits, such as exercising, meditating, or immersing oneself in nature. Foster self-compassion and exhibit kindness to oneself when confronted with setbacks or disappointments.

5. Reframe Negative Thoughts: Negative thoughts and self-talk can hinder our progress and make us feel stuck. To overcome negative thoughts, practice reframing them into more positive, empowering statements. For example, instead of "I can't do this," reframe it as "I haven't mastered this yet, but with practice and dedication, I will get there."

6. Stay Flexible: Life is unpredictable, and it's important to stay flexible and adaptable when faced with obstacles and challenges. Be willing to adjust your goals and plans when necessary and remain open to new opportunities and possibilities.

Although it can be uncomfortable and arduous, change is frequently a prerequisite for personal growth and development. Embrace change as a chance for growth and education and concentrate on the advantages it can offer.

In summary, to triumph over obstacles and transcend challenges, one must utilize a combination of perspective, tactics, and assistance. By adopting a growth-oriented mindset, establishing achievable objectives, seeking guidance, practicing self-care, transforming pessimistic thoughts, embracing change, and maintaining flexibility, it is possible to surpass barriers and advance towards your aspirations and ambitions. Keep in mind that hurdles and challenges are opportunities for personal development and education, and with perseverance and resolve, any obstacle can be overcome.

PART VI

DEVELOPING RESILIENCE
AND MINDFULNESS

In today's fast-paced world, people are faced with numerous challenges that can cause stress, anxiety, and other mental health issues. Developing resilience and mindfulness can help individuals cope with these challenges and become more mentally and emotionally strong. In this chapter, we will explore the concept of resilience and mindfulness, their benefits, and how they can be developed.

The resilience is the capacity to recover from adversity and overcome challenges. It entails adapting to changes and handling stress with competence. Resilience is not an inherent trait but rather a learned skill that can be improved through practice and experience. Strengthening resilience can boost an individual's emotional intelligence, problem-solving abilities, and overall well-being.

Mindfulness entails being entirely engaged and present in the current moment without any judgment. It encompasses observing one's thoughts, feelings, and physical sensations. Mindfulness practice has been demonstrated to alleviate stress, enhance emotional control, and boost concentration and attentiveness. Mindfulness can be cultivated via mindfulness meditation, which entails sitting calmly and concentrating on one's breath.

Developing resilience and mindfulness has a multitude of advantages. Individuals who possess these traits are more adept at handling stress and setbacks, and they are less susceptible to mental health disorders like depression and anxiety. Furthermore, they are more likely to cultivate positive relationships with others, exhibit higher levels of work productivity, and experience greater overall contentment in life.

There are various methods and techniques for developing resilience and mindfulness. These may include engaging in regular physical exercise, maintaining healthy eating habits, keeping a journal, practicing gratitude, and participating in mindfulness meditation. It is crucial to identify the practices and techniques that are most effective for everyone, as everyone has distinct preferences and requirements.

In subsequent sections, we will investigate methods and exercises for fostering resilience and mindfulness. By integrating these practices into their everyday routines, individuals can enhance their general sense of well-being and cultivate greater resilience and mindfulness when confronted with life's obstacles.

CHAPTER ELEVEN

THE VALUE OF RESILIENCE AND MINDFULNESS IN PERSONAL GROWTH

The advancement of oneself through self-reflection, education, and the acquisition of new abilities characterizes personal growth. The cultivation of resilience and mindfulness can be crucial for personal growth, as it empowers individuals to surmount challenges and enhance self-awareness. This chapter will examine the significance of resilience and mindfulness in personal growth.

Resilience is a crucial component of personal growth as it allows individuals to bounce back from setbacks and failures. It provides individuals with the ability to face challenges head-on and persevere through difficult times. When individuals develop resilience, they are better equipped to handle difficult situations and adapt to changes. This allows for personal growth to occur as individuals are more willing to take risks, try new things, and push themselves out of their comfort zones.

Mindfulness is also an essential component of personal growth. Mindfulness allows individuals to become more self-aware, gain perspective, and become more present in their daily lives. When individuals practice mindfulness, they are better able to understand their thoughts and emotions, which can lead to improved decision-making and communication skills. This, in turn, can lead to personal growth as individuals become more aware of their own strengths and weaknesses, and develop the skills to improve themselves.

Resilience and mindfulness work together to facilitate personal growth. When individuals are faced with challenges or setbacks, they can use mindfulness to become aware of their thoughts and emotions, and then use resilience to overcome those challenges. This allows individuals to learn from their experiences and develop new skills and strategies for future challenges.

Additionally, developing resilience and mindfulness can also lead to greater self-acceptance and self-love. When individuals practice mindfulness, they are more aware of their own thoughts and emotions and can learn to accept themselves for who they are. This can lead to increased self-confidence and a greater sense of self-worth, which can facilitate personal growth.

In conclusion, developing resilience and mindfulness can be incredibly valuable for personal growth. When individuals develop these skills, they become better equipped to face challenges, adapt to change, and become more self-aware. By incorporating resilience and mindfulness into their daily lives, individuals can experience greater personal growth and become the best version of themselves.

CHAPTER TWELVE

RESILIENCE AND MINDFULNESS TECHNIQUES AND EXERCISES

Developing resilience and mindfulness requires consistent practice and dedication. In this chapter, we will explore specific techniques and exercises that can help individuals develop resilience and mindfulness.

Resilience Techniques:

1. Reframing: This technique involves changing one's perspective on a situation to see the positive aspects. For example, instead of focusing on the negative aspects of a difficult situation, individuals can focus on the opportunities for growth and learning that the situation presents.

2. Establishing Social Support: Forming a network of encouraging friends and family members can aid in constructing resilience. When individuals possess a support system to rely on during arduous periods, they are better equipped to manage challenges and recuperate from disappointments.

3. Self-Care: The practice of self-care can assist individuals in cultivating resilience by alleviating stress and improving overall well-being. Self-care practices can involve ensuring adequate sleep, adhering to a balanced diet, and engaging in routine exercise.

Mindfulness Techniques:

1. Mindful Breathing: This technique involves focusing on the breath and bringing attention to the present moment. To practice mindful breathing, individuals can sit in a quiet space and focus on their breath, taking deep breaths in and out and noticing the sensation of the breath in their body.

2. Body Scan: The body scan technique involves bringing attention to different parts of the body and noticing any sensations that are present. To practice body scanning, individuals can lie down and bring attention to different parts of their body, starting with their toes and moving up to their head.

3. Mindful Walking: Mindful walking involves bringing attention to the present moment while walking. Individuals can practice mindful walking by focusing on the sensation of their feet touching the ground, the movement of their body, and the sounds and sights around them.

Incorporating these techniques and exercises into daily life can help individuals develop resilience and mindfulness. It is important to remember that developing these skills takes time and dedication, and individuals should be patient with themselves as they work towards their goals. By consistently practicing these techniques, individuals can become more resilient and mindful, leading to greater overall well-being and personal growth.

PART VII

CREATING A SUPPORTIVE COMMUNITY

In today's world, which can often feel alienating and fragmented, creating and cultivating communities that provide support has become increasingly vital. Such communities consist of people who join forces to assist one another, exchange insights, and collaborate towards shared objectives. Whether it is a social circle, a business network, or a civic association, supportive communities can offer individuals a sense of kinship, direction, and contentment.

This chapter is a guide to creating and sustaining supportive communities. In this chapter we will explore the benefits of supportive communities, as well as strategies and practices for building and nurturing them. We will also discuss common challenges that can arise in building and maintaining supportive communities and provide guidance on how to overcome them.

The upcoming sections of this book will encompass various themes, ranging from the significance of communication and trust in creating supportive communities to techniques for fostering an atmosphere of inclusivity and diversity. Additionally, we will delve into diverse kinds of supportive communities, such as online communities and groups centered around particular interests or objectives.

This chapter is intended for individuals who aspire to create and nurture supportive communities, whether in personal or professional contexts. Whether you are a community leader, a community member, or someone who wishes to learn more about fostering supportive communities, this section will provide you with the essential information and tools to make a positive impact on your own life and the lives of others.

Creating a supportive community is a rewarding and fulfilling experience that can bring individuals together, foster meaningful relationships, and contribute to overall well-being. We hope that this book will inspire and empower you to create and nurture supportive communities in your own life and beyond.

Section 1: Communication and Trust – Cornerstones of Supportive Communities

In today's world, where individuals are often struggling with various challenges, building and nurturing supportive communities has become increasingly important. Such communities can provide individuals with a sense of belonging, purpose, and well-being, ultimately leading to a more fulfilling life. However, the foundation of any supportive community lies in the establishment of effective communication and trust.

a. Communication

Communication is vital in any relationship, and this holds true for the creation of supportive communities. Effective communication helps build trust, fosters a sense of belonging, and ensures that everyone's needs and desires are heard and acknowledged. Open and honest communication allows individuals to express themselves freely and voice their concerns, which can help prevent misunderstandings and conflicts.

b. Active Listening

Active listening is an essential component of communication within a supportive community. It involves fully engaging in the conversation, focusing on what the speaker is saying, and seeking to understand their perspective. Active listening requires individuals to set aside their own biases and judgments and approach the conversation with an open mind. By actively listening, individuals can demonstrate that they value and respect the opinions and feelings of others, which can help build trust within the community. Ultimately, active listening plays a crucial role in fostering a supportive environment where individuals feel heard and understood.

c. Trust

Trust is another crucial aspect of creating supportive communities. Trust is built over time and through consistent behavior. Trust is fostered when individuals are reliable, follow through on their commitments, and act in the best interest of the community. When individuals trust each other, they feel more comfortable being vulnerable and sharing their experiences and emotions. This vulnerability leads to deeper connections and a stronger sense of community.

d. Psychological Safety

Psychological safety is an essential aspect of creating a supportive community, and it is crucial to build trust and improve communication. It involves feeling comfortable expressing oneself without the fear of negative consequences such as judgment or punishment. Individuals are more likely to share their thoughts and ideas openly when they feel psychologically safe, leading to innovative insights and solutions.

Section 2: Fostering Inclusivity and Diversity in Supportive Communities

Today, diversity and inclusivity are essential for the creation of supportive communities. A community that celebrates and embraces diversity, and creates an inclusive environment, can offer individuals a sense of belonging, acceptance, and support. However, creating such an atmosphere requires intentionality and deliberate action. In this chapter, we will explore techniques for fostering an atmosphere of inclusivity and diversity in supportive communities.

1. Educate and Raise Awareness: Education and awareness are the foundation for creating an inclusive and diverse community. By learning about different cultures, backgrounds, and perspectives, individuals can develop a deeper understanding and appreciation for diversity. Additionally, raising awareness about various issues affecting marginalized communities can help create a more inclusive environment.

2. Create Safe Spaces: Creating safe spaces is critical for individuals who may have experienced discrimination or harassment in the past. Safe spaces provide a sense of security and comfort and allow individuals to express themselves freely without fear of judgment or retribution. Safe spaces can be physical locations or virtual spaces, such as online forums or social media groups.

3. Encourage Diversity in Leadership: Diversity in leadership is critical for creating an inclusive community. When individuals from diverse backgrounds and experiences hold leadership positions, they bring unique perspectives and insights to the table. Encouraging diversity in leadership positions also sends a message that the community values and celebrates diversity.

4. Celebrate Diversity and Cultural Events: Celebrating diversity and cultural events is an

excellent way to foster an inclusive and diverse community. Celebrating cultural holidays, hosting cultural events, and inviting individuals from diverse backgrounds to share their experiences can help build bridges and create connections between different communities.

5. Implement Inclusive Policies: Creating and implementing inclusive policies is essential for creating an environment where everyone feels valued and respected. Inclusive policies can include nondiscrimination policies, and accommodations for individuals with disabilities

6. Create Opportunities for Dialogue: Creating opportunities for dialogue allows individuals to share their thoughts, feelings, and experiences. Dialogue helps build empathy and understanding and can create a sense of community. Creating opportunities for dialogue can be as simple as hosting community meetings or creating online forums where individuals can share their perspectives.

In conclusion, creating an inclusive and diverse community requires intentionality and deliberate action. Educating individuals, creating safe spaces, encouraging diversity in leadership, celebrating diversity and cultural events, implementing inclusive policies, and creating opportunities for dialogue are all techniques that can help foster an atmosphere of inclusivity and diversity in supportive communities. By prioritizing these techniques, we can create communities that celebrate diversity and offer individuals a sense of belonging, acceptance, and support.

Section 3: Types of Supportive Communities

Supportive communities come in many forms, each with its unique advantages and disadvantages. Some communities form around shared interests, while others arise from a common need for support. In this chapter, we will explore different types of supportive communities, including online communities, interest-based communities, and goal-oriented communities.

1. Online Communities: Online communities have become increasingly popular in recent years, thanks to the widespread availability of the internet. These communities can take various forms, such as social media groups, online forums, or chat rooms. Online communities offer individuals the opportunity to connect with others from around the world, regardless of geographic location. They also provide a sense of anonymity, which can be comforting for individuals who may feel more comfortable sharing personal information online rather than in person. However, online communities also have their drawbacks, such as the potential for miscommunication or lack of accountability.

2. Interest-Based Communities: Interest-based communities bring individuals together around a common interest or hobby. These communities

can take many forms, from book clubs to fan groups to sports teams. Interest-based communities provide individuals with a sense of camaraderie and can help individuals feel more connected to others who share their passions. They also offer opportunities for personal growth and learning, as individuals can share knowledge and expertise with one another. However, interest-based communities can sometimes become insular, leading individuals to focus exclusively on their shared interests and neglect other aspects of their lives.

3. Goal-Oriented Communities: Goal-oriented communities form around a shared objective or goal, such as a fitness group or a business networking group. These communities offer individuals the opportunity to work towards a common objective while receiving support and encouragement from others. Goal-oriented communities can provide individuals with a sense of accountability and motivation, making it easier to achieve their objectives. However, they can also be competitive, leading individuals to compare themselves to others rather than focusing on their own progress.

4. Local Communities: Local communities are formed around geographic location, such as a neighborhood or town. These communities offer individuals the opportunity to connect with others who share their geographic location, fostering

a sense of community and belonging. Local communities can also provide individuals with support in times of need, such as during a natural disaster or a personal crisis. However, local communities can also be insular, leading individuals to exclude those who are perceived as outsiders.

In conclusion, supportive communities come in many forms, each with its unique advantages and disadvantages. Online communities, interest-based communities, goal-oriented communities, and local communities all offer individuals the opportunity to connect with others and receive support. By understanding the diverse types of supportive communities, individuals can choose the type that best fits their needs and preferences.

CHAPTER THIRTEEN

RECOMMENDATIONS FOR BUILDING A COMMUNITY OF SUPPORT

Building a community of support can be a challenging but rewarding process. In this chapter, we will provide recommendations for creating a supportive community that is inclusive, welcoming, and effective.

1. Establish Clear Goals and Objectives: It is important to establish clear goals and objectives for your community, so that everyone understands the purpose and mission of the group. This will help to ensure that everyone is working towards the same goals and will make it easier to measure the success of the community.

2. Foster Open Communication: Open communication is essential for building a supportive community. Encourage members to express their opinions, ideas, and concerns, and create a space where everyone feels heard and valued. Regular check-ins and meetings can help to facilitate open communication.

3. Create a Culture of Trust: Trust is critical for building a supportive community. Establishing clear expectations, following through on commitments, and being transparent in your actions can help to foster a cul-

ture of trust. Encourage members to share their experiences and support one another and provide opportunities for feedback and input.

4. Prioritize Inclusivity and Diversity: Creating a community that is inclusive and diverse can help to foster a sense of belonging and support for all members. Consider how to make your community accessible to a variety of individuals, and actively seek out diverse perspectives and experiences.

5. Encourage Personal Growth and Development: A supportive community should be focused on helping members grow and develop, both personally and professionally. Encourage members to share their skills and expertise and provide opportunities for learning and growth.

6. Flexibility and adaptability: Both are crucial when building a supportive community, as the process is continuous, and circumstances can change. Being receptive to innovative ideas and suggestions and being prepared to modify your approach when necessary is essential.

To sum up, the establishment of a supportive community is a potent approach to nurture a feeling of connectedness, assistance, and overall wellness. Adhering to these suggestions can aid in crafting a community that is all-encompassing, efficient, and helpful, ultimately leading to a constructive influence on the people in your surroundings.

PART VIII

TAKING ACTION AND MAKING A DIFFERENCE

The challenges of today's world can leave us feeling powerless and overwhelmed. With issues such as climate change and social inequality, it can be difficult to see how we can make a positive impact. However, there is still hope. This chapter provides valuable insights into effective strategies for taking action and creating meaningful change, both in our personal lives and in the broader world. Through exploring these strategies, we can empower ourselves to make a real difference and contribute to a brighter future for all.

This chapter delves into effective strategies for discovering our passions and sense of purpose, taking small steps towards change, speaking up for what we believe in, and cultivating empathy and compassion in our efforts to bring about positive change. Regardless of whether our interests lie in environmental activism, social justice, or community building, this chapter equips us with practical tools and strategies to make a tangible impact on the world.

The central theme of this chapter is empowerment – the understanding that every individual has the potential to cultivate constructive transformation, regardless of magnitude. By working together and taking action, we can construct a world that is fair, sustainable, and impartial for all. Let us commence on this expedition of exploration and explore the various avenues through which we can make a significant difference and bring about optimistic change.

CHAPTER FOURTEEN

MAKING A POSITIVE CHANGE IN THE WORLD

As individuals, we possess an innate desire to leave a positive impact on the world we inhabit. Be it through our personal connections, professional endeavors, or contributions to community initiatives, we strive to effect meaningful change. This chapter delves into a range of effective strategies for bringing about positive transformations in the world.

1. Discover Your Passion and Purpose: To create a meaningful impact, it is essential to first identify your areas of passion and purpose. What drives you? What causes are close to your heart? By gaining clarity on these aspects, you can channel your energy towards bringing about positive change in those specific areas.

2. Start Small: Making a positive change in the world can seem overwhelming, but it is important to remember that small actions can have a big impact. Start by identifying small, achievable goals that align with your passions and purpose. For example, you might volunteer at a local organization or start a community group focused on a specific issue.

3. Collaboration and teamwork: Both are often necessary to bring about positive change. Connecting with individuals who share your interests and goals is essential, and seeking opportunities to work together can be beneficial. This may involve joining a community group or getting involved in a social movement.

4. Use Your Voice: Your voice is a powerful tool for creating positive change. Use social media, letters to elected officials, and other forms of communication to raise awareness about the issues you care about. Encourage others to get involved and share their perspectives as well.

5. Practice Empathy and Compassion: Creating positive change in the world requires empathy and compassion. Try to understand the perspectives and experiences of others and approach your efforts with a spirit of kindness and empathy.

6. Be Persistent and Patient: Creating positive change can be a slow and challenging process. Be persistent in your efforts, even when progress seems slow, and practice patience as you work towards your goals.

In conclusion, making a positive change in the world is not always easy, but it is a deeply fulfilling and rewarding experience. By identifying your passions and purpose, starting small, connecting with others, using your voice, practicing empathy and compassion, and being persistent and patient, you can create a positive impact in the world around you.

CHAPTER FIFTEEN

STRATEGIES FOR MAKING A DIFFERENCE AND IMPACTING THE WORLD

Making a difference and impacting the world requires a deep sense of passion and purpose. It is essential to identify what truly matters to you and what drives you to make a change. Start by reflecting on your values, strengths, and experiences. Ask yourself questions such as:

- What issues in the world do I care about the most?
- What skills and talents do I possess that can be used to make a difference?
- What experiences have I had that have inspired me to take action?
- What kind of impact do I want to make in the world?

Once you have a clear sense of your passion and purpose, you can begin to develop strategies for making a difference and impacting the world.

Educating Yourself

Before you can make a difference, you must educate yourself about the issues you care about. Research the history and current state of the issue, the relevant laws and policies, and the perspectives of different stakeholders. Seek out diverse sources of information, including academic research, news articles, and personal stories.

In addition to educating yourself about the issue, it is also essential to develop a deep understanding of the communities and individuals affected by it. This may involve listening to their stories, attending community meetings, and volunteering with organizations that are working to address the issue.

Finding Your Purpose

The first step in making a difference and impacting the world is to identify your purpose. It's important to understand what you care about and what motivates you. Ask yourself: what is important to me? What problems do I want to solve? What skills do I have that can be used to make a difference? Once you've identified your purpose, you can then start thinking about the strategies you can use to make an impact.

Identify the Issues

Once you know what you care about, it is important to identify the issues that need to be addressed. Conduct research and gather information about the issue you want to tackle. Look at the causes and effects of the issue and identify the stakeholders involved. Understanding the problem is crucial to developing effective strategies to address it.

Set Realistic Goals

Setting goals is important when working towards making a difference. Set clear, measurable goals that are specific, realistic, and achievable. This will help you track your progress and stay motivated.

Develop a Strategy

With your purpose, issues, and goals in mind, it is time to develop a strategy. Identify the tactics you can use to address the issues and achieve your goals. This may involve collaborating with other individuals or organizations, fundraising, creating awareness through social media or organizing events, and other methods that align with your values and goals.

Building Relationships and Collaborating with Others

Making a difference and impacting the world often requires working collaboratively with others. Building relationships with individuals and organizations that share your passion and purpose can help you to amplify your impact and achieve your goals.

Look for opportunities to collaborate with others in your community or field. Attend networking events, join organizations, and volunteer with groups that are working towards similar goals. Be open to learning from others and be willing to share your own knowledge and expertise.

Taking Action

Putting your plans into action is the most crucial step towards making a difference and impacting the world. After identifying your passion and purpose, educating yourself about the issue, and building relationships with others, acting becomes imperative.

Develop a clear plan of action that outlines your goals, strategies, and timeline. Be willing to adapt your approach as needed and to learn from your successes and failures along the way. Remember that making a difference often requires persistence, patience, and a willingness to take risks.

Measuring Your Impact and Celebrating Your Successes

Finally, it is essential to measure your impact and celebrate your successes along the way. This will help you to stay motivated and continue to be effective over the long term.

Develop metrics for measuring your impact, such as the number of people you have reached, the policy changes you have influenced, or the positive outcomes you have achieved. Celebrate your successes with your team and community and use them as motivation to continue your work.

In conclusion, making a difference and impacting the world requires passion, purpose, education, collaboration, action, and celebration. By following these strategies, you can achieve your goals and create a positive impact on the world.

Strategies for Creating a Plan of Action

1. **Set a specific and measurable goal:** Identify a specific and measurable goal that you want to achieve. Make sure that it is realistic and achievable within a specific timeframe.

2. **Break down the goal:** Break down your goal into smaller, achievable steps. This will help you to see progress and stay motivated along the way.

3. **Determine resources:** Determine the resources you need to achieve your goal, such as time, money, and people. Identify potential barriers or obstacles that may hinder your progress.

4. **Develop a timeline:** Develop a timeline for achieving each step of your goal. Assign specific dates or deadlines for each task.

5. **Identify possible strategies:** Identify possible strategies for achieving your goal. Brainstorm different approaches that align with your values and goals.

6. **Select an approach:** Select the approach that aligns best with your values and goals, and that you believe is most likely to help you achieve your goal.

7. **Create an action plan:** Create an action plan that outlines the steps, resources, timeline, and strategies that you will use to achieve your goal. Be specific and detailed, and make sure that the plan is realistic and achievable.

8. **Monitor and evaluate progress:** Monitor your progress regularly and evaluate whether you are on

track to achieve your goal. If you encounter any obstacles, adjust your plan as needed.

In conclusion, it is important to celebrate your successes, even the small ones, as you work towards your goal. Doing so will help you stay motivated and continue to make progress.

With these steps, you can develop a plan of action that will enable you to accomplish any goal, be it related to personal growth, career, education, health, or any other area of your life. Keep your attention, motivation, and dedication fixed on your goal, and remain open to change and adaptable when necessary.

Self-Acknowledgment Tools and Tips for Women

1. **Start a gratitude journal:** Write down three things you are grateful for each day. It could be as simple as having a roof over your head or a supportive friend.

2. **Practice positive self-talk:** Incorporate positive self-talk into your routine by using kind and encouraging words towards yourself and taking time to reflect on your strengths and past achievements.

3. **Celebrate your success:** Make sure to recognize and appreciate your accomplishments, regardless of how insignificant they may appear, by taking the time to celebrate them.

4. **Surround yourself with positivity:** Foster a positive environment by surrounding yourself with individuals who provide encouragement and support, while minimizing interactions with those who have a negative impact on your well-being.

5. **Engage in self-care:** Prioritize your holistic well-being by engaging in self-care activities that promote physical, emotional, and mental health. This may include regular exercise, mindfulness practices such as meditation or yoga, and engaging in hobbies or activities that bring you joy and relaxation.

6. **Set boundaries:** Establish healthy boundaries by recognizing and communicating your limits. Say "no" to commitments or activities that do not align with your values or goals and assert your needs with individuals who may not respect your boundaries.

7. **Seek feedback:** Gaining insights into your strengths and areas for improvement can be beneficial by soliciting feedback from people you trust, like friends, family, or colleagues.

8. **Embrace imperfection:** It's important to accept imperfection and recognize that making mistakes is a normal part of being human.

9. **Focus on progress, not perfection:** Shift your focus from pursuing perfection to making progress. Remember to acknowledge and celebrate every small step you take as it brings you closer to achieving your goal.

10. **Cultivate self-compassion:** Cultivate self-compassion by extending to yourself the same kindness and understanding you would give to a dear friend experiencing a difficult time.

Tips for Women on a Significant Step Towards Improving Personal Growth:

1. **Identify your strengths and weaknesses:** Understanding your strengths and areas for improvement can help you develop a plan for personal growth.

2. **Set clear goals:** Setting specific, measurable, achievable, relevant, and time-bound (SMART) goals can help you stay focused and motivated.

3. **Learn new skills:** Pursue activities or courses that interest you and can help you develop new skills or improve existing ones.

4. **Embrace failure and mistakes:** Making mistakes and experiencing failure is part of the growth process. Embrace them as opportunities for learning and improvement.

5. **Nurture your physical, emotional, and mental well-being:** Prioritize activities that help you feel your best, such as regular exercise, mindfulness practices like meditation or yoga, and spending quality time with the people you care about.

6. **Seek feedback and constructive criticism:** Asking for feedback from trusted sources can provide valuable insights and help you grow.

7. **Get out of your comfort zone:** To cultivate personal growth, it is beneficial to challenge yourself by embracing novel and daring experiences beyond your comfort zone. This can enhance your resilience and self-confidence. Explore uncharted territories to expand your horizons.

8. **Reflect on your experiences:** Regularly reflect on your experiences and what you have learned. This can help you stay on track towards your goals and continue growing.

In conclusion, remember, personal growth is a journey, not a destination. It takes time and effort, but the rewards are worth it. By taking these tips to heart, you can set yourself up for a successful and fulfilling journey towards personal growth.

Tips and Steps for Women to Find a New Purpose in Life:

1. **Assess your current situation:** Start by assessing where you currently are in life. What are your strengths and weaknesses? What makes you happy and fulfilled? What do you want to change? Be honest with yourself and identify areas that need improvement.

2. **Identify your values:** Determine what values are important to you. What principles do you want to live your life by? Knowing your values can help you prioritize your goals and make decisions that align with your beliefs.

3. **Explore new interests:** Accept new hobbies or explore interests you've always been curious about. Trying new things can expand your horizons and expose you to different perspectives.

4. **Volunteer:** Engaging in volunteer work for a cause you are passionate about cannot only create a sense of purpose for you but also have a positive impact on your community. Additionally, it can help you meet new people and acquire new skills.

5. **Reflect on your past experiences:** Think about times in your life when you felt fulfilled or accomplished. What made those experiences meaningful? Can you apply those elements to your current situation?

6. **Take action:** Don't be afraid to take action towards your new purpose. It can be scary to step outside of your comfort zone, but it is necessary for personal

growth. Remember that progress takes time and effort.

7. **Seek support:** Talk to trusted friends or family members about your journey. Consider working with a therapist or coach to help you navigate any challenges you may encounter.

In conclusion, after gaining a clearer understanding of what you desire, establish achievable goals to strive for. For larger objectives, divide them into smaller, more attainable steps.

It is important to remember that discovering a new purpose is a unique and personal journey. Allow yourself to be patient and celebrate small accomplishments as you progress.

Tips and Strategies for Women to Achieve Empowerment:

1. **Define what empowerment means to you:** Empowerment can mean different things to different people. Take some time to think about what it means to you and what areas of your life you want to feel empowered in.

2. **Build self-confidence:** Work on building your self-confidence by identifying your strengths and accomplishments. Practice positive self-talk and avoid negative self-talk.

3. **Develop assertiveness skills:** Learn to express your needs and opinions in a clear and respectful way. Practice saying "no" when necessary and setting boundaries.

4. **Invest in education and skills:** Invest in education and skills that can help you achieve your goals. This could be through formal education or attending workshops and trainings.

5. **Strong Support System:** To foster a dedicated support system, it is important to surround yourself with individuals who are encouraging and supportive, including friends, family, and colleagues. Additionally, seek out guidance and inspiration from mentors and role models who can provide valuable insights and advice.

6. **Advocate for yourself and others:** Speak up for yourself and others in situations where your rights or

dignity are being threatened. This could be in the workplace, at home, or in the community.

7. **Embrace you:** Embrace your individuality and celebrate the qualities and characteristics that make you unique. Do not hesitate to be true to yourself and pursue your passions.

8. **Resilience:** Develop your resilience by using setbacks and challenges as opportunities to learn and grow. Cultivate a growth mindset that focuses on finding solutions instead of dwelling on problems.

In conclusion, develop your resilience by using setbacks and challenges as opportunities to learn and grow. Cultivate a growth mindset that focuses on finding solutions instead of dwelling on problems.

Self-discovery is an important process for personal growth and development. Here are some tips and strategies for women to embark on their own self-discovery journey:

1. **Investing Time:** Investing time in introspecting your values and acknowledging what holds the greatest importance to you can give you the power to make informed decisions and lead a more fulfilling life.

2. **Explore your interests:** Try new things and engage in activities that you enjoy. This can help you discover your passions and purpose.

3. **Spend time alone:** Take some time to be alone with your thoughts and feelings. This can help you get in touch with your inner self and gain clarity.

4. **Journaling:** Write down your thoughts, emotions, and experiences. This can help you gain insights into yourself and your life.

5. **Feedback:** Gather feedback by approaching people you trust, such as friends, family members, or colleagues, and request candid evaluations of your strengths and weaknesses. This process can assist you in recognizing areas that need improvement and further developing your strengths.

6. **Mindfulness:** Nurture mindfulness by fully focusing on the present moment and watching your thoughts and emotions without any negative judgment. This technique can heighten your self-awareness and empower you to handle your emotions more efficiently.

7. **Practice self-care:** Take care of yourself physically, emotionally, and mentally. This can help you build resilience and maintain a positive mindset.

In conclusion, always keep in mind that self-discovery is a journey, not a destination. As you explore and discover more about yourself, be kind, patient, and compassionate towards yourself.

EPILOGUE

EMBRACING YOUR METAMORPHIC JOURNEY

The journey of the metamorphic woman is one of growth, transformation, and empowerment. It is a journey that requires resilience, courage, and a willingness to embrace change. Throughout this book, we have explored the various stages of the metamorphic journey, from awakening to integration. We have seen how women can overcome their limiting beliefs, redefine their identities, and create fulfilling and meaningful lives.

But the journey does not end here. Embracing your metamorphic journey means recognizing that growth and change are ongoing processes. It means continuing to push yourself outside of your comfort zone, to learn from your experiences, and to embrace new opportunities.

As you progress on your path, keep in mind the importance of treating yourself with kindness and patience. While change can bring about discomfort and difficulty, it is crucial for your individual development and metamorphosis. It is advisable to seek the company of individuals who are encouraging, who have faith in your capabilities, and who can assist you in overcoming obstacles.

Lastly, keep in mind that your transformative expedition is distinct to you. There is no universal approach to personal growth and metamorphosis. Embrace your distinctiveness, appreciate your capabilities, and leverage them to generate a favorable influence on the world.

In conclusion, the metamorphic woman is a powerful force for change and transformation in the world. By embracing your journey and continuing to push yourself forward, you can create a life that is fulfilling, meaningful, and full of purpose.

Bibliography

1. Adams, S. (2019). Embracing Change and Taking Risks: A Guide to Personal and Professional Growth. New York: Penguin Random House.

2. The Power of Mindset by Carol S. Dweck (2017). New York: Random House.

3. Gladwell, M. (2019). The tipping point: How little things can make a big difference. Back Bay Books.

4. Heath, C., & Heath, D. (2017). The power of moments: Why certain experiences have extraordinary impact. Simon & Schuster.

5. Hill, N. (2019). Overcoming Obstacles to Personal Growth and Development. Positive Psychology.

6. McMillan, D. W., & Chavis, D. M. (1986). Sense of community: A definition and theory. Journal of community psychology, 14(1), 6-23.

7. Minkler, M. (2012). Community organizing and community building for health and welfare. Rutgers University Press.

8. Rogers, M. (2020). The Power of Self-Confidence and Self-Esteem: A Guide to Cultivating a Positive Self-Image. New York: HarperCollins.

9. Senge, P. (2006). The necessary revolution: How individuals and organizations are working together to create a sustainable world. Broadway Business.

10. Southwick, S. M., Bonanno, G. A., Masten, A. S., Panter-Brick, C., & Yehuda, R. (2014). Resilience definitions, theory, and challenges: Interdisciplinary perspectives. European Journal of Psychotraumatology, 5(1), 10.3402/ejpt.v5.25338

ACKNOWLEDGEMENTS

I feel immense gratitude for the support of numerous individuals who aided me throughout the process of authoring this book.

Primarily, I want to thank God for providing me with the inspiration and guidance to author this book. Your love and grace have sustained me through all the difficulties of this process.

Additionally, I extend my gratitude to my children for serving as a continuous source of inspiration and delight. Your limitless inventiveness and vitality serve as a reminder of the significance of maintaining a curious and receptive mindset.

I am deeply grateful to my dear friends and family, whose unwavering support has been a constant source of strength throughout my journey. Your love and encouragement mean the world to me, and I treasure them greatly. I am truly fortunate to have such a remarkable group of individuals in my life.

About the Author

Roxanne is an enthusiastic writer and researcher with a degree in Psychology. Her love for writing and research has been a lifelong passion that has led her to write various children's educational workbooks and the children's book series Lilia and Max's School Adventures.

As a curious and analytical thinker, Roxanne enjoys exploring different topics and is especially interested in understanding the human mind and behavior. This has led her to pursue a degree in psychology, where she has developed critical thinking skills that are evident in her writing.

Besides her passion for writing and research, Roxanne possesses an ardent desire to assist others and make a meaningful contribution to her community. She actively participates in community service and has volunteered for a range of organizations over the years.

Music has also played a significant role in Roxanne's life, and she has a great appreciation for its power to uplift and inspire. She believes that music can connect people from all social classes and to bring them together in a positive and peaceful environment.

As an advocate for women's empowerment, Roxanne is enthusiastic about helping women reach their full potential at any age. She believes that education and personal growth are key to achieving success, even in the face of challenges and setbacks. Her interest in women's progress has led her to start her own software company, where she uses her newly acquired skills as an app developer to support her local Native community as well as help individuals and businesses fulfil their dream of owning their own app. In addition, Roxanne is an entrepreneur of various online businesses.

During her leisure time, she indulges in painting and creating art, which enables her to unleash her creativity and unwind her mind. Her optimistic approach to life and her faith and strength she finds in God of positivity are evident in all her creative writing.

As the author of this book, Roxanne would like her readers to understand that her faith in God is the foundation of everything she does. It is through her relationship with Him that she has gained the strength, courage, and wisdom to navigate life's challenges and pursue her passion for writing. She firmly believes that God has given her a purpose and a message to share with the world, and this book is a manifestation of His grace and love for all of us. Her hope is that as you read these words, you will be inspired and reminded of the power and goodness of God, who is the ultimate source of all things.